WEATHER MAKES THEM MOVE

DRAGONFLY MIGRATION

by Rachel Rose

Consultant: Beth Gambro
Reading Specialist, Yorkville, Illinois

Minneapolis, Minnesota

Teaching Tips

Before Reading
- Look at the cover of the book. Discuss the picture and the title.
- Ask readers to brainstorm a list of what they already know about dragonflies. What can they expect to see in this book?
- Go on a picture walk, looking through the pictures to discuss vocabulary and make predictions about the text.

During Reading
- Read for purpose. Encourage readers to think about dragonfly movement as they are reading.
- Ask readers to look for the details of the book. Why do dragonflies migrate?
- If readers encounter an unknown word, ask them to look at the sounds in the word. Then, ask them to look at the rest of the page. Are there any clues to help them understand?

After Reading
- Encourage readers to pick a buddy and reread the book together.
- Ask readers to name a reason dragonflies move. Find a page that tells about this thing.
- Ask readers to write or draw something they learned about dragonfly migration.

Credits:
Cover and title page, © Brian E. Kushner/Shutterstock; 3, © Hintau Aliaksei/Shutterstock; 5, © donna apsey/EyeEM/Adobe Stock; 7, © Stefan Rotter/iStock; 8–9, © blackdiamond67/Adobe Stock; 10–11, © Rita Priemer/Adobe Stock; 13, © Patrick Rolands/Shutterstock; 15, © Praiwan Wasanruk/iStock; 17, © youm118/Shutterstock; 18–19, © Pobytov/iStock; 20–21, © chermit/Adobe Stock; 22T, © Pavlov Sergei888/Shutterstock; 22B, © Rob Hainer/Shutterstock; 23TL, © wavebreakmedia/Shutterstock; 23TM, © Malgorzata Surawska/Shutterstock; 23TR, © Stefan Rotter/iStock; 23BL, © Robert Ross/Shutterstock; 23BM, © Brian A Jackson/Shutterstock; 23BR, © jorgriommi/iStock.

Library of Congress Cataloging-in-Publication Data

Names: Rose, Rachel, 1968- author.
Title: Dragonfly migration / by Rachel Rose.
Description: Minneapolis, Minnesota : Bearport Publishing Company, [2024] |
  Series: Weather makes them move | Includes bibliographical references
  and index.
Identifiers: LCCN 2022059171 (print) | LCCN 2022059172 (ebook) | ISBN
  9798888220641 (hardcover) | ISBN 9798888222621 (paperback) | ISBN
  9798888223796 (ebook)
Subjects: LCSH: Dragonflies--Migration--Juvenile literature. |
  Dragonflies--Seasonal distribution--Juvenile literature.
Classification: LCC QL520 .R68 2024 (print) | LCC QL520 (ebook) | DDC
  595.7/331568--dc23/eng/20221215
LC record available at https://lccn.loc.gov/2022059171
LC ebook record available at https://lccn.loc.gov/2022059172

Copyright © 2024 Bearport Publishing Company. All rights reserved. No part of this publication may be reproduced in whole or in part, stored in any retrieval system, or transmitted in any form or by any means, electronic, mechanical, photocopying, recording, or otherwise, without written permission from the publisher.

For more information, write to Bearport Publishing, 5357 Penn Avenue South, Minneapolis, MN 55419.

Contents

Time to Go 4

On the Move! 22
Glossary 23
Index 24
Read More 24
Learn More Online 24
About the Author 24

Time to Go

A little dragonfly **hovers** by a pond.

The weather is changing.

Now, the **insect** must leave.

Why does it have to go?

Dragonflies live all around the world.

Many make their home in North America.

During the summer, some live in the more northern parts.

There, the summer weather is warm.

But then the **seasons** change.

It gets colder.

Dragonflies cannot live in the cold.

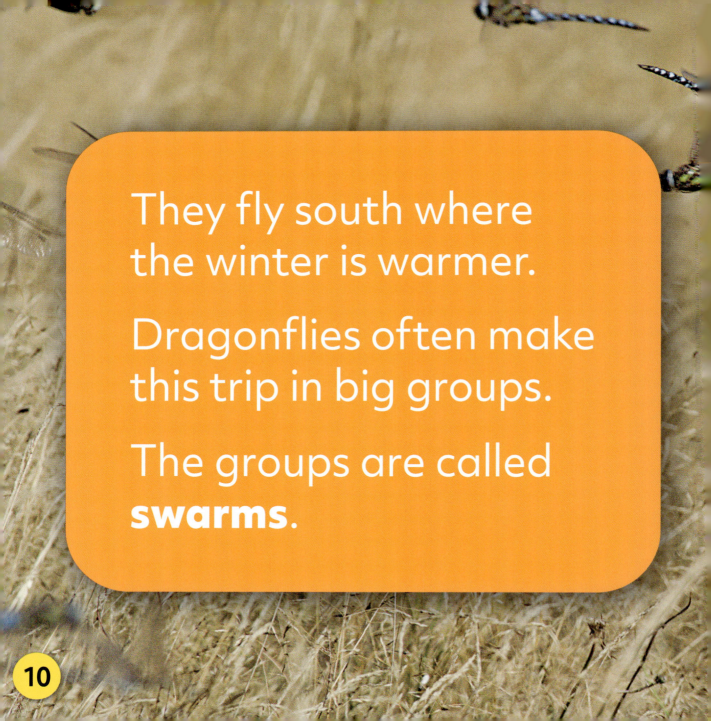

They fly south where the winter is warmer.

Dragonflies often make this trip in big groups.

The groups are called **swarms**.

Once they get there, the dragonflies lay eggs.

Then, they die.

Most dragonflies live for only about eight weeks.

Soon, the eggs **hatch**.

A new **generation** grows.

They become adults.

These dragonflies spend their whole lives in the south.

Say generation like *jen*-uh-RAY-shuhn

When spring comes, they lay eggs and die.

Even more dragonflies hatch from their eggs.

By this time, it is warmer.

The young dragonflies follow the warm weather.

It is time to fly north.

Dragonflies make this trip every year.

It is all because weather makes them move!

On the Move!

Migration (mye-GRAY-shuhn) is when animals move from one place to another. Often, they travel far. Let's learn more about dragonfly migration!

Some dragonflies fly more than 1,500 miles (2,400 km).

The third generation of dragonflies knows where to go in the north. This is even though they have never been there.

Glossary

generation a group of people or animals born around the same time

hatch to come out of an egg

hovers stays in one place in the air

insect a small animal with three body parts and six legs

seasons the parts of a year with different weather

swarms large groups of dragonflies flying together

Index

adults 14
cold 8
eggs 12–14, 16
north 6, 19, 22
season 8
south 10, 14
swarms 10
warm 8, 10, 19

Read More

Carr, Aaron. *Dragonflies (Everything about Bugs).* New York: AV2, 2022.

Jaske, Julia. *I See Dragonflies (Bugs in My Backyard).* Ann Arbor, MI: Cherry Lake Publishing, 2022.

Learn More Online

1. Go to **www.factsurfer.com** or scan the QR code below.
2. Enter **"Dragonfly Migration"** into the search box.
3. Click on the cover of this book to see a list of websites.

About the Author

Rachel Rose is a writer who lives in California. She is not a big fan of bugs, but she does like dragonflies.